HOW TO DRAW
KINGS &
QUEENS

David Antram

BOOK HOUSE
Aberdeenshire

Published in Great Britain in MMXVIII by
Book House, an imprint of
The Salariya Book Company Ltd
25 Marlborough Place, Brighton BN1 1UB
www.salariya.com

ISBN: 978-1-912006-89-2

1 3 5 7 9 8 6 4 2

A CIP catalogue record for this book is available
from the British Library.

Printed and bound in China.

Author: **David Antram** was born in Brighton,
England, in 1958. He studied at Eastbourne College
of Art and then worked in advertising for fifteen
years before becoming a full-time artist. He has
illustrated many children's non-fiction books.

Editor: Nick Pierce

Visit
www.salariya.com
for our online catalogue and
free fun stuff.

**WARNING: Fixatives should be used
only under adult supervision.**

Note on text:
Dates given refer to length of reign.

Contents

Making a start

Learning to draw is about looking and seeing. Keep practising and get to know your subject. Use a sketchbook to make quick drawings. Start by doodling, and experiment with shapes and patterns. There are many ways to draw, and this book shows only some of them. Visit art galleries, look at artists' drawings and see how friends draw, but above all, find your own way.

Mary, Queen of Scots
1542–1567

Queen Alexandra
1901–1910

James II
1685–1688

Edward VII
1901–1900

George III
1760–1820

Queen Anne
1702–1714

King William III
1689–1702

Queen Mary II
1689–1694

Edward VI
1547–1553

Robert the Bruce
1306–1329

5

Drawing tools

Here are just a few of the many tools that you can use for drawing. Let your imagination go, and have fun experimenting with all the different marks you can make.

Pencil

Watercolour pencil

Charcoal pencil

Charcoal stick

Pastels

Finger painting

Black, grey and white pastel on grey sugar paper

Each grade of **pencil** makes a different mark, from fine, grey lines through to soft, black ones. Hard pencils are graded as H, 2H, 3H, 4H, 5H, and 6H (the hardest). An HB pencil is ideal for general sketching. Soft pencils are graded from B, 2B, 3B, 4B, 5B to 6B (the softest and blackest).

Watercolour pencils come in many different colours and make a line similar to an HB pencil. But paint over your finished drawing with clean water, and the lines will soften and run.

It is less messy and easier to achieve a fine line with a **charcoal pencil** than a stick of charcoal. Create soft tones by smudging lines with your finger. **Ask an adult** to spray the drawing with fixative to prevent further smudging.

Pastels are brittle sticks of powdered colour. They blend and smudge easily and are ideal for quick sketches. Pastel drawings work well on textured, coloured paper. **Ask an adult** to spray your finished drawing with fixative.

Experiment with **finger painting**. Fingerprints make exciting patterns and textures. Use your fingers to smudge soft pencil, charcoal and pastel lines.

Ballpoint pens are very useful for sketching and making notes. Make different tones by building up layers of shading.

A **mapping pen** has to be dipped into bottled ink to fill the nib. Different nib shapes make different marks. Try putting a diluted ink wash over parts of the finished drawing.

Draughtsmen's pens and specialist **art pens** can produce extremely fine lines and are ideal for creating surface texture.
A variety of pen nibs are available which produce different widths of line.

Felt–tip pens are ideal for quick sketches. If the ink is not waterproof, try drawing on wet paper and see what happens.

Broad–ribbed **marker pens** make interesting lines and are good for large, bold sketches. Try using a black pen for the main sketch and a grey one to block in areas of shadow.

Paintbrushes are shaped differently to make different marks. Japanese brushes are soft and produce beautiful flowing lines. Large sable brushes are good for painting washes over a line drawing. Fine brushes are good for drawing delicate lines.

Ballpoint pen

Mapping pen

Draughtsman's pen

Felt–tip pen

Marker pen

Paintbrush

7

Materials

Try using different types of drawing paper and materials. Experiment with charcoal, wax crayons and pastels. All pens, from felt-tips to ballpoints, will make interesting marks — or try drawing with pen and ink on wet paper.

Felt-tip

Oliver Cromwell
1653–1658

Cromwell became Lord Protector of England after the English Civil War. The war ended in 1651 and Charles I was executed. Cromwell ruled via a Republican form of government until his death in 1658.

Ink silhouette

King John
1199–1216

King John inherited the throne of England from his brother, Richard the Lionheart in 1199. He sealed the Magna Carta, which guaranteed the rights of the English nobility.

Queen Anne
1702–1714

Pencil

Queen Anne was the last monarch of the House of Stuart, dying without an heir in 1714. Having struggled through 18 pregnancies she failed to produce a child who lived beyond its youth. Her reign saw four great British victories in battle against Spain during the War of the Spanish Succession. This led to the establishment of Britain as a formidable European power.

Charles II
1660–1685

Pen and ink

Despite being king in name, Charles II had to wait for the restoration of the monarchy in 1660 before he could reclaim the throne. Although he pursued a life of pleasure, keeping many mistresses, he had a keen interest in science and architecture. His good looks and controversial lifestyle made him popular with his subjects.

9

Proportions

Heads are difficult shapes to draw. The face includes some of the most expressive features of the body. Using construction lines helps you to place the eyes, nose, ears and mouth accurately before you start drawing the head in more detail.

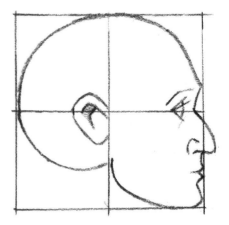

Side view

Establish the main shape of the head by overlapping two ovals.

The eyes are positioned at the midpoint of the head. Note the position of the ears in relation to the eyeline.

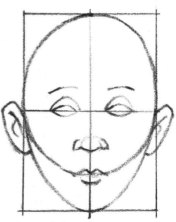

Frontal view

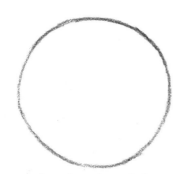

Construction lines help you to accurately place the facial features.

When drawing the head from different angles, construction lines are particularly useful in helping you to keep the features in the correct positions.

Use downward curving construction lines to show the head looking downwards.

Elizabeth I
1558–1603

Use upward curving construction lines to show the head looking up.

Erase all unwanted construction lines.

11

William The Conqueror

1066–1087

W illiam I, usually known as William The Conqueror, was a Norman. The Normans invaded England in 1066 and ruled the country for 88 years. In 1086, William ordered the compilation of the Domesday Book, which recorded landowners who owned and farmed the land, and assessed the value of their property.

Start by drawing a large oval for the torso and two small ovals for the head and hips. Add lines for the arms and legs with dots for the joints. Indicate the eyeline and position of William's sword.

Using the construction lines as a guide, start to add shape to the body. Indicate the knee and elbow joints. Draw his fingers and facial features. Add the platform he's seated on, and his sword.

Now add further details, including William's hair, throne, the blade and hilt of his sword, and the folds of his robe and cloak. Add steps at his feet.

This seated position emphasises the regal identity and authority of the king.

Add all final details and shading to areas that are darker in tone or in shadow.

Reversing out

Create impact in a simple line drawing by reversing it out as a white line on a black background.

Erase all unwanted construction lines.

13

Richard I

1189–1199

Known as Richard Coeur de Lion, meaning 'Lionheart', Richard I spent very little time in England as he was fighting abroad for most of his reign. Richard led the third crusade (1189–92 AD) with Philip II of Spain against the Muslim forces of Saladin, Sultan of Egypt and Syria.

Start by drawing ovals and circles for Richard's head, torso and hips. Then add his arms and legs with dots for the joints. Now sketch in his horse in the same way. Indicate the position of William's eyeline and that of his horse. Add William's sword held aloft.

Add shape to Richard's limbs and torso, as well as the body of his horse. Sketch in Richard's saddle, sword hilt and facial features. Add the horse's ears, eyes, nostrils and mouth.

14

Sketch in Richard's facial features and his beard and helmet. Add more detail: his sword blade, his chainmail and the folds and shape of his tunic. Draw the horse's hood, coat, harness and bit.

Draw close lines to suggest the weave of the chainmail. Sketch in the emblem on Richard's tunic and complete all final details and shading.

Motion lines

You can create a sense of motion by placing abstract lines around the figure or object in your drawing.

Erase all unwanted construction lines.

Henry VI

1422–1461
1470–1471

Henry VI was born in 1421 AD and succeeded to the throne in 1422 at the age of just eight months! During his reign he lost most of the English land in France, with only Calais remaining under English rule. He eventually lost the crown when the Yorkists claimed his throne.

Start by drawing ovals and circles for the head, torso and hips. Add a centre line, then add the arms with ovals for the hands. Sketch in the position of Henry's sword and his facial features.

Draw in cylinder shapes for his arms with circles to indicate joints. Sketch in his facial features, hair and crown. Indicate the shapes of his armour.

Now start defining the shapes that make up Henry's suit of armour, including all straps and fastenings. Add jewels to his crown and draw in the blade and hilt of his sword.

Add all finishing touches and shading. Areas where light doesn't reach will be darkest. Leave parts of your drawing white to represent the highlights on Henry's armour.

Add a sharp point to Henry's sword, and rivets in his armour.

Erase all unwanted construction lines.

17

Richard III

1483–1485

Richard III was the last of the Plantagenet dynasty and the last king of the House of York. He was killed at the Battle of Bosworth Field in 1485, making him the last English king to die in battle on English soil. His remains were found under a Leicester car park in 2012, and he was reburied in Leicester cathedral.

Richard III

Richard III had a spinal condition which probably gave him a hunched posture.

As an adolescent, Richard developed scoliosis, curvature of his spine.

Draw a circle for the head and construction lines (as shown) to help position Richard's facial features and chin.

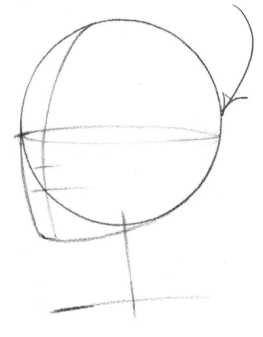

Now draw in the eyes, eyebrows, nose, mouth and ears.

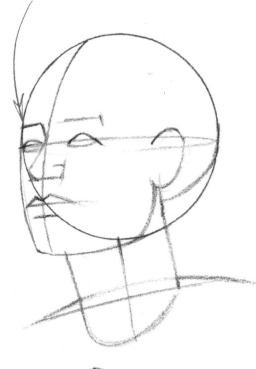

Sketch in the shape of Richard's hat and its decorative jewels. Draw in his hair and add detail to his face.

Add shading to areas that are darker in colour or in shadow. Finish off all final details of Richard's clothes and face.

Erase all unwanted construction lines.

Henry VIII

1509–1547

Henry VIII was born in 1491 and succeeded to the throne in 1509. He had six wives during his lifetime. Henry was infuriated when the head of the Catholic Church, the Pope, refused to allow him to divorce his first wife, Catherine of Aragon. So Henry broke with the church and made himself the head of the Church of England. He went on to have six wives during his lifetime and died in 1547.

Start by drawing in three ovals for the head, torso and hips. Then add lines for the arms and legs with dots for each joint. Indicate the position of Henry's facial features and sketch in simple shapes for his feet.

Use cylinder shapes to draw in the arms and legs with circles at each joint. Join together the hip and chest areas of the torso. Add facial features and shaping to the hands.

Now start dressing the King. Draw in the shapes of his tunic, top coat, feathered hat, and shoes. Sketch in Henry's fingers, his jewellery, and his dagger and hilt. Draw in his beard and start to add any shading.

Finish off all the finer details of Henry's elaborate outfit. Include all patterns, fastenings and the Tudor fashion of 'slashed' sleeves. Add more shading to areas that are darker in colour or in shadow. Use a scribbly shading to differentiate textures like the fur lining of his topcoat.

Erase all unwanted construction lines.

21

James I

1603–1625

James I, born in 1566, was King James VI of Scotland before he succeeded to the English throne in 1603. In 1605, Guy Fawkes and his fellow Catholic conspirators planned an attempt on James' life with their plot to blow up Parliament. James ordered a new translation of the Bible from Latin into English, the version still used today.

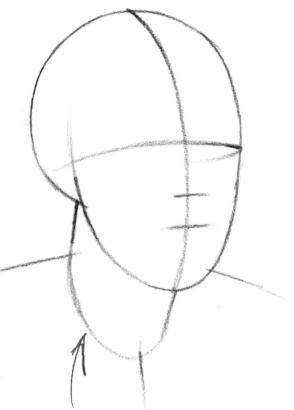

Draw an overlapping circle and oval for James' head. Add construction lines to help position his facial features.

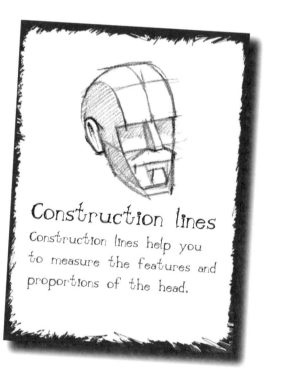

Construction lines

Construction lines help you to measure the features and proportions of the head.

Draw in his eyes, eyebrows, nose, mouth, ears, hair and his neck ruff.

Darken James' eyes but leave a small white highlight in each one. Draw in the shape of his moustache and beard. Add shading to his face and hair to indicate the light source direction.

Use a single jagged line to start building up the layers that form James' ruff.

Add more shading to give texture and definition to the hair, beard and ruff.

Suggest the layered ruff with lots of overlapping jagged, scribbly lines.

Erase all unwanted construction lines.

George IV

1820–1830

George IV as a young man.

Having already spent nine years as Prince Regent under his father, George III, whose health had deteriorated, George IV finally inherited the throne in 1820. He was known for leading a debauched and hedonistic lifestyle.

Start by drawing in two ovals and a circle for the head, torso and hips. Add arms and legs with dots for the joints. Indicate the position of George's facial features. Sketch in the chair he's sitting on and add simple shapes for his hands and feet.

Draw a large circle for George's bulging stomach and use cylinder shapes for his legs and arms. Add his facial features and hair and define the shape of his hands. Draw in the chair legs and the shape of his chair and the tabletop alongside.

Start adding detail to George's clothing: his waistcoat, jacket, breeches, shoe buckles and stockings. Draw in his fingers, the cigar he's holding and the items on the table beside him.

The facial expression is crucial to indicate the personality of your subject.

Complete the final details. Include all the fold lines of his clothing curving around his large body. His button-popping breeches and gaping waistcoat emphasise his girth. Shade in areas that are darker in colour or in shadow. Draw in the folded drapery of the tablecloth.

Erase all unwanted construction lines.

Queen Victoria

1837–1901

Penny coin featuring Queen Victoria

Victoria was only 18 years old when she succeeded to the throne, but she immediately embraced the duties and responsibilities of her position. Her long reign of almost 64 years saw the industrialisation of Britain and its ascent to becoming the most powerful empire the world had known. Her reign was marked by a long period of public mourning after the sudden death of her husband, Prince Albert, in 1861.

Draw a series of circles for the coin (as shown). Place a vertical and a horizontal construction line through the centre to help position Victoria's head. Draw in the shape of her head in profile.

Now sketch in Victoria's eyes, nose, mouth, ears and hair. Add small lines around the edge to correctly position the letters on the coin.

Add more detail to Victoria's face, including locks of hair and the shape of her eyes. Sketch in the lettering and add a date to the coin.

Now add shading to suggest texture and to add definition.

Don't forget to add small indentations around the circumference of the coin.

Erase all unwanted construction lines.

Queen Elizabeth II

1952–

Elizabeth II is now the longest–reigning monarch in British history. She has sat on the throne from the years of austerity following the Second World War into the early decades of the 21st century. She is a hugely popular and iconic figure around the world.

Start by drawing in ovals for the head, torso and hips. Then add the arms and legs with dots for the joints. Indicate the position of Elizabeth's facial features, her throne and sceptre.

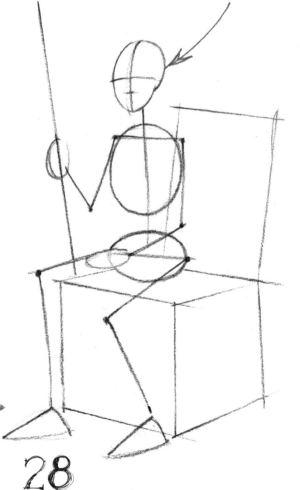

Use cylinder shapes for her arms and legs. Draw in the shape of Elizabeth's dress and cloak, her crown, the ball–shaped orb in her hand and the decoration on her sceptre. Sketch in her eyes, nose, mouth and ears.

28

Start adding more detail: first sketch in Elizabeth's hair, crown, sceptre and throne with its lion-headed armrests. Add her fingers and draw in the draped folds of her robes. Sketch in the tassels and ribbons on the cloak and add detail to the sceptre and orb.

Add black tips to the cloak's white ermine trim.

Now complete all details. Add shading to areas that are darker in colour and also to evoke the different textures of Elizabeth's coronation robes.

Sketch in all patterns to Elizabeth's dress and robes.

Erase all unwanted construction lines.

The Crown Jewels

The Crown Jewels of the United Kingdom, including St Edward's Crown, are kept in the Tower of London. They are protected by a state-of-the-art security system and visited by thousands of tourists each year.

Draw in the basic shapes of St Edward's Crown. Construction lines in the form of ellipses will help you to accurately position the decorative bands of precious gems.

The 'Honours' of Scotland, the Scottish Crown Jewels, are the oldest royal regalia in Britain. The crown dates from before 1540, when James V ordered its remodelling.

Add the three visible curved arches that support the orb and cross. Sketch in the fleur-de-lys shapes embedded with precious stones.

Embellish the cross and orb with jewels. Note the free hanging pearls at either side.

Start adding detail to the crown jewels. Add the many gold balls that decorate the circumference of the base, and the arches of the crown. Sketch in the soft folds of the velvet inset and indicate the texture of the fur trim.

The inset cap is made of purple velvet and is trimmed with ermine.

Add shading to areas that are darker in colour, like the purple velvet cap and also areas in shadow. Use shading to create different textures, too. Leave some areas white like the top edges of the fur and for highlights in the jewels and gold surfaces.

Erase all unwanted construction lines.

31

Glossary

Composition   The arrangement of the parts of a picture on the drawing paper.

Construction lines   Guidelines used in the early stages of a drawing; they may be erased later.

Light source   The direction from which the light seems to come in a drawing.

Negative space   The empty space between parts of a drawing, often an important part of the composition.

Proportion   The correct relationship of scale between each part of the drawing.

Silhouette   A drawing that shows only a flat dark shape, like a shadow.

Index